Horrid Halloween

Poems about Halloween and Halloween celebrations for young children

Hadley James

Contents

Part 1: Halloween Party

Part 2: Poems for Halloween

Part 1
Halloween Party

Halloween Party

It's Halloween, hip hip hooray,
We're ready to party all night,
The house is decorated the pumpkins
 are ready,
Shining with flickering light.

The creatures are waiting,
To come out and play,
They can't wait to party,
It's their favourite day.

They are all very different,
But like to have fun,
Please join us inside,
To meet everyone ...

Gertie Ghost

I have a white shape,
I have dark eyes,
I give everyone,
An enormous surprise.

I like to float,
Here and there,
We Ghosties can go,
Everywhere!

BOO!

Wally Werewolf

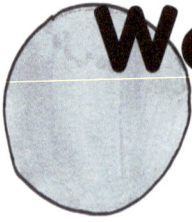

I look quite normal,
Most of the time,
A little bit hairy,
But that's just fine.

When the moon is full,
I let out a howl,
The wolf takes over,
It makes me...

... GRRRRRROWL!

Wanda Witch

I have a broom,
And a pointy black hat,
I like to cast spells,
And spend time with my cat.

We go out at night,
On my broom for a fly,
We zoom around,
And touch stars in the sky.

Mike Mummy

I have lots of bandages,
But no broken bones,
My arms are stuck out,
I like to groan.

But the thing that I find,
Really quite funny,
Is everybody calls me Mummy...

.....When actually I'm a Daddy!

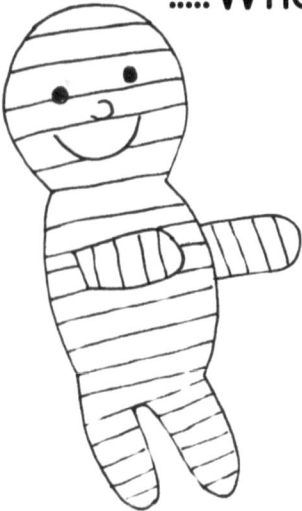

Valentino Vampire

I have very sharp fangs,
I like to drink blood,
I wake up at night,
I think everyone should!

I'm not keen on garlic,
I don't like the sun,
But I do like to party,
And have lots of fun!

Zelda Zombie

Grr argh!
Brains are yummy.
Grr argh!
Get brains in my tummy.

Grr argh!
I need to eat.
Grr argh!
Your Brains are a treat!

Seb Skeleton

Dem bones, dem bones,
They help me dance and run,
Dem bones, dem bones,
Help me leap and have fun.

Just because my bones
have no skin,
It makes my friends jump,
When they see my big grin.

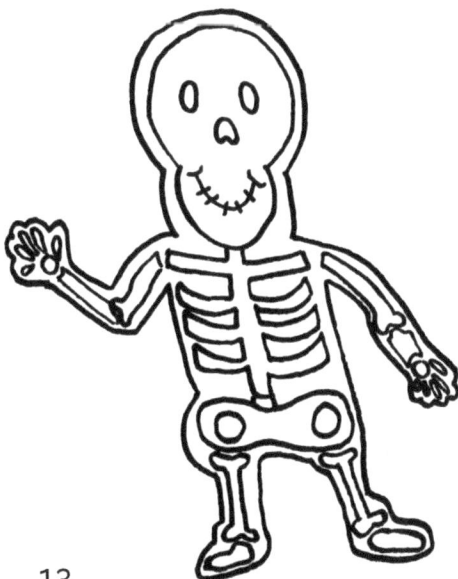

Boris Bat

My name is Boris Bat,
I love to fly at night,
I swoop through the air,
And give you a fright.

I like to hang around,
And be upside down,
When people see my fangs,
They run out of town.

Jimmy Jack-o'-lantern

I have a pointed smiling mouth,
I'm lit from the inside,
When the ghouls and ghosts come
out to play,
I shine my light with pride.

My smile is fixed upon my face,
I wake up when it's night,
If you saw me out walking,
It might give you a fright!

Wizard Wade

I have a bushy moustache,
I have a long white beard,
I have a purple flowing cape,
Some people think I'm weird.

I like to cast funny spells,
My Magic is on trend,

I use a spell book and my wand,
To astonish all my friends.

Part 2

Poems for Halloween

Happy Halloween

It's the 31st of October,
The day we've been waiting for,
The costumes are all ready,
We can't wait to get out the door.

I've got my basket in one hand,
My broomsticks in the other,
There's me, a werewolf, a zombie, a
ghost,
And a vampire that looks like my
brother.

We go to the houses with lights on,
With decorations galore,
We take a deep breath and step
forward,
Then someone knocks on the door.

"Trick or Treat!" we say together,
The people in the house smile,
Our buckets fill up and we're
grateful,
We walk for about a mile.

We go home tired and weary,
I'm yawning but still very glad,
I've got enough sweets to last all
year,
This is the best Halloween I've had!

A Recipe for Halloween

Take a spoonful of excitement,
Add a pinch of fun,
Find some scary costumes,
Then our recipe has begun.

Mix some ghouls and ghosties,
Stir in a bat and cat,
Add a cup of cobwebs,
And a pointed Witches hat.

Select your greatest ever tricks,
Then add a bag of treats,
Sprinkle in some laughter,
And a pinch of something sweet.

Put it in a cauldron,
Add one more bag of tricks,
Then spread the magic everywhere,
For the perfect Halloween mix.

Hooray for Halloween

H ere it is,
A ll Hallows Eve,
L et's have lots of fun,
L et's put on our costumes,
O r get the house decorating done,
W hen it is Halloween,
E veryone can see,
E verybody all around,
N ow has as much fun as can be!

Witches Brew

Get the cauldron ready,
Make sure that it's hot,
Let the water bubble,
So, it's ready in the pot.

Eye of newt,
Foot of frog,
Shell of snail,
Mud from a bog.

Tail of mouse,
Toe of rat,
Skin of snake,
Wing of bat.

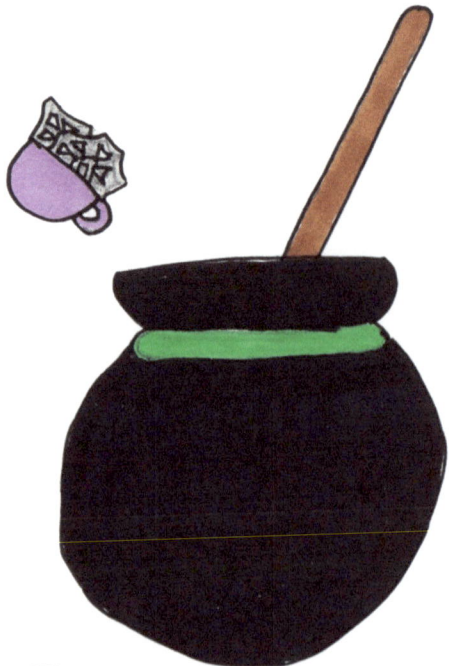

Mix it up,
Stir it in,
Let it bubble,
Then begin.

Put it in a goblet,
Drink it in one go,
Say the magic words,
Then let's start the show!

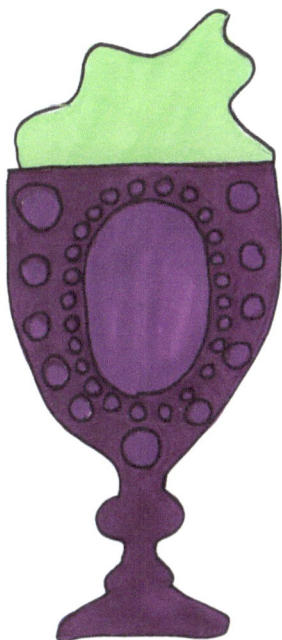

Spooky Stories

There was a house in a dark town,
It was abandoned and completely run down.

There was a ship that had no crew,
It drifted on the sea so blue.

There was a girl with a doll that spoke,
It ran away and her heart broke.

There was a house as haunted as can be,
There were ghosts around for all to see.

There was a dog who felt so sad,
His owner died and he felt bad.

It's Halloween night we gather round,
To tell spooky stories that we have found.

Which Witch?

The red witch likes to ride her broom,
The purple witch drives a car that zooms.

The yellow witch likes to play ball,
The green witch gives her friends a call.

The blue witch likes to have a party,
The orange witch is very arty.

The silver witch likes to cook,
The gold witch likes to read a book.

The white witch likes to dance and play,
The black witch likes to sing all day.

Each witch has something they love to do,
Which witch is your favourite, please tell
me who?

Boo!

White sheet,
Cut out eyes,
Who's under there?
It's a surprise!

The sheet is big,
Goes to the ground,
Ready to get treats,
From all around.

Careful walking,
Don't want to trip,
It's been raining,
Don't want to slip.

Lots of houses,
Lots of treats,
Think I have,
My weight in sweets!

Back home,
Take off my shoe,
Jump out on Mum,
Shouting "Boo!"

BOO!

Trick or Treat

The night is here!
Ready everyone,
I 'm in my costume,
Come on let's have some fun,
Kids are walking everywhere,
On a mission to find treats,
Ready with their favourite tricks,
Then they can have some sweets,
Right now the street is busy,
Everyone is having fun,
And then it's time to go back home,
To share what we have done!

Wicked Witch

She wears a pointed hat,
She rides upon a broom,
She has a fluffy cat,
She likes to see the moon.

She has a big black cauldron,
She likes to cast a spell,
She likes to tend her garden,
She has a wishing well.

She has a pointed nose,
She never seems to smile,
She likes to wear black clothes,
She thinks it's a good style.

I'm not sure that she's wicked,
She just likes to be alone,
She takes care of her garden,
And looks after her home.

A Mummy Mishap

"Who stole all the toilet roll?"
My Mum yells out,
Then she comes in,
And gives a great shout.

My brother is wrapping me up,
The loo roll goes round and round,
I'm going to look amazing,
The best Mummy in town.

I'm all wrapped up and ready,
But there's something I don't see,
The Mummy's disappearing,
I'm turning back into me.

By the time we get to the second house,
I'm leaving a trail behind,
No one has noticed anything yet,
But we're very easy to find.

We get to the fourth house and get lots of treats,
This truly is very good fun,
Then we realise I'm unravelling,
I retrace my steps at a run!

I gather my loo roll bandages up,
Following where we have been,
I'm looking a bit dishevelled,
The very worst Mummy you've seen!

Magic Potion

Hubble, bubble, there's going to be
trouble,
It's Halloween tonight,
Let's make a magic potion,
To give everyone a fright!

A potion to make us invisible,
A potion to make us fast,
A potion so that we can fly,
A potion that will last.

I gather the ingredients,
I stir them in so well,
I gulp the magic potion down,
And hope it all goes well!

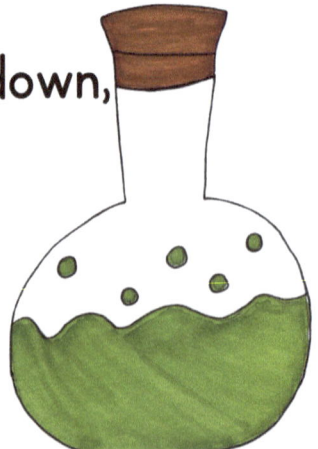

Haunted House

We always run past,
That one house on our street,
People say it's haunted,
By things you don't want to meet.

There are cobwebs in the
doorways,
A cat upon the path,
The trees groan in the wind,
To protest against its wrath.

No one ever goes inside,
But at night the lights are on,
It is completely empty,
But the ghosts all party on!

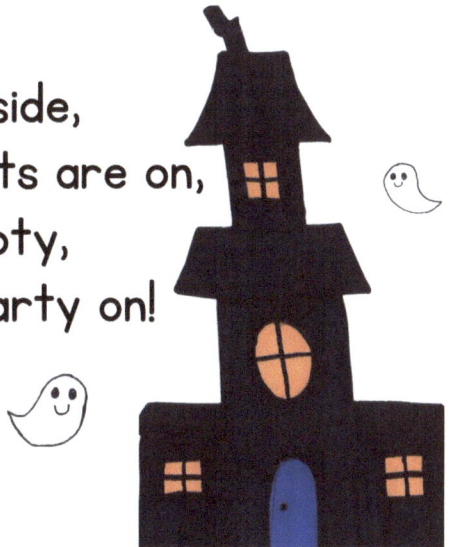

Ghost Train

Train ride,
Let's go,
What will we see?
We don't know!

Dark tunnel,
Spider web,
Groaning noise,
Above my head.

Glowing eyes,
Curdling scream,
Can't believe,
What we've just seen!

Day light,
Back outside,
Let's go for,
Another ride!

Witchy Wishes

I wish I was a witch,
I'd ride upon a broom,
I'd dance round the stars,
And fly around the room.

I'd make a lot of mischief,
I'd cast a lot of spells,
I'd cook in a cauldron,
And create lots of bad smells.

I'd have a black cat,
I'd cackle with glee,
I'd have so much fun,
You would all envy me!

Midnight

It's midnight on Halloween,
The spookiest night of the year,
The witches and skeletons come out
to dance,
The ghouls and ghosties are near.

We dress up and celebrate,
We've all had lots of fun,
But now it's time to snuggle
down,
The partying is done.

Now it is the witching hour,
You should be tucked in bed,
To dream of happy endings,
While the ghosts dance
 round your head.

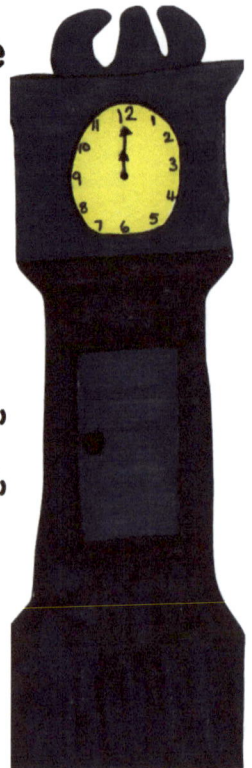

36

Also by Hadley James:

Wonderful Me

Hadley James

Autumn Days

Hadley James

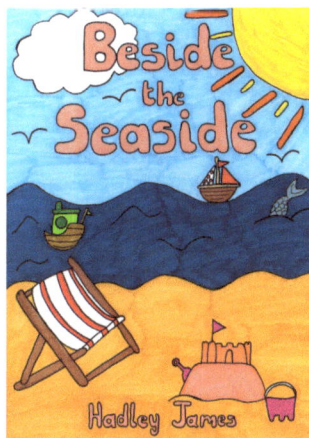

Beside the Seaside

Hadley James

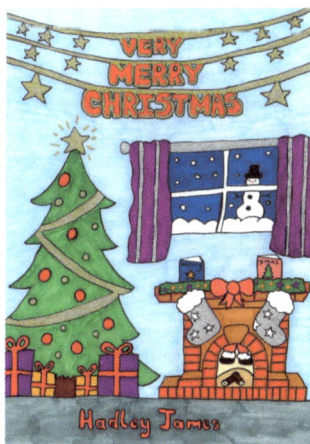

VERY MERRY CHRISTMAS

Hadley James

Wonderful Winter
Hadley James

Spectacular Spring
Hadley James

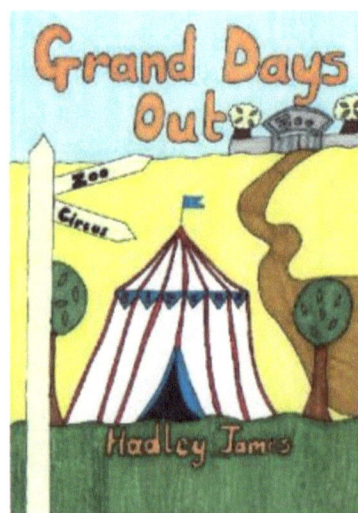

Grand Days Out
Zoo
Circus
Hadley James

Extreme Environments
Hadley James

Summer Dreams
Hadley James

Marvellous Minibeasts
Hadley James

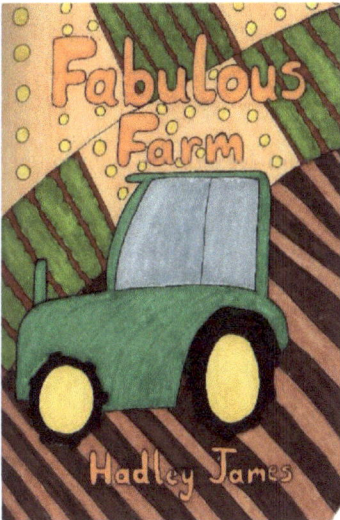
Fabulous Farm
Hadley James

www.ingramcontent.com/pod-product-compliance
Lightning Source LLC
Chambersburg PA
CBHW041803040426
42448CB00001B/28